VOID AND COMPENSATION

MICHAEL MORSE

CANARIUM BOOKS
ANN ARBOR, MARFA, IOWA CITY

SPONSORED BY
THE HELEN ZELL WRITERS' PROGRAM
AT THE UNIVERSITY OF MICHIGAN

VOID AND COMPENSATION

Canarium Books
Ann Arbor, Marfa, Iowa City
www.canarium.org

The editors gratefully acknowledge the
Helen Zell Writers' Program at the University of Michigan
for editorial assistance and generous support.

Cover photograph:
James Casebere, *Venice Ghetto*, 1991
© James Casebere
Courtesy of the artist and Sean Kelly Gallery, New York

First Edition

Printed in the United States of America

ISBN 13: 978-0-9849471-7-1

CONTENTS

Void and Compensation (4)

Void and Compensation (5)

Grace fills empty spaces, but it can only enter where there is a void to receive it, and it is grace itself which makes this void.

Simone Weil

And Place was where
the Presence was
Circumference between

Emily Dickinson

I know not what to say.
I will not swear these are my hands. Let's see:

Lear

VOID AND COMPENSATION (1)

(Karaoke Genesis)

Since when did keeping things to ourselves ⟩
help us to better remember them?

We need tutorials from predecessors.

To restore what's missing makes a science
of equating like with like, or touching
small pebbles on a larger mental abacus.

We hitch a memory of order to ourselves:

from rotating bodies in space comes wind,
by which we're buffeted, cooled, or graced;
The sun warms both the sunflower
and the angel with whom we might wrestle;
We get some lyrics from a higher power
and then we act on or for each other.

In calculated reunions of broken parts,
the latter must always feel the former,
inherit both the track and the turn.

A situation like an empty orchestra.

And when we try to sing above it, intuit,
and even in our singing are mistaken—

if pitch is something sought and never pure,
if latter sounds like something we can climb

as opposed to where we find ourselves
more recently in our relations, in time,
having been left or starting our leave-taking—

something happened—someone followed someone.
Someone had. Even held. Our formers.

We're doppelgängers, saintly or undone;
pick a song and listen for your cue.

Here's the void. Now sing some compensation. ✓

(Eponym Imperfect)

April, the meadowlark back on his post
with ex-cathedra powers of speech—
sing-song fence-sitter, he lets his wishes rip.
The pairing off in earnest has begun.
Spring-loaded and girl-crazy, he flares
his yellow belly, shouts out to reel them in.
Up above, blue sky and kestrel hover,
his flutter hunt a little more proactive.

I would carry the eponym *imperfect*
and still wake to gold-stick willows ready
to shake up and green-leave the good world.
I'd walk a sun-willing creek and think
that what the world spends the Hawthorne suffers;
sometimes up empty and sometimes sated
the kestrel and his hover hunt will come.

It's in the very bones of larks to sing
and song's an exponential reckoning
of skyward intentions *if I were, I would*.
Brave subjunctive bird, what on earth will do?

.

(My Ear, My Alabama, My Monk)

Here comes Thelonious weather, all elbows and knees
and in-between notes—a virtuoso thirst

of clouds now tattering big blue and down
come colored leaves who've left their lives as shades.

Harbingers, the notes scurry like small children
who in their cravings tend to disfigure themselves.

My ear, my Alabama, and my Monk:

my single malt, my Talladega wren,
part winglet, part malfeasant, flirting

with the narrator and making of the riff-
raff an armada of ready sophists.

His play limns a weather of fevered unthinking. ✓

Close your eyes. Let the junks on the river *Dream*
play détente, drift into view from left to right.

(No "I" in Team)

I've been told by dozens of angry men
that the name on the front of my jersey
is significantly more important
than the name sewn on my back.

Little compensations of detachment—
I'm an early draft pick, a team player.

I am a Brewer. A Dodger. A Red.

the group and
the indiv.

Fidelity investments: I have
aggressive funds and little gain.

She who walks with me has no name on her back:
free agent, are you betraying or betrayed? ✔
Are you obsessed with leaving or left out?

Angel, Mariner, Oriole,
I want strikes for the heart of the order,
a game face so I might suffer preferences.

Sun breaks through clouds—Giant consequences.

Whom shall I call? How shall I pitch to them?

(Tsimtsum)

[handwritten: God withdraws to make th spae for th world]

[handwritten: ✓ C] Years go by without your mother's voice, without her
on the other end of a voice.

Perpetual Yom Kippur. You don't practice. You fast.

You've got a bone chip in your pocket and a song to pick.

She was young and beautiful with her satchel of wishes and cloves.

She preferred cocktails over weeping; wisteria for the lock,
stock, and barrel; thin graphite for a *Bildungsroman*.

And then a child.

Any kind mothering's a *tsimtsum*:
a contraction of self, a withdrawal

that allows for making,

a falling back into nothing you can name.

Put a junebug in a cup and call it Petrarch.
Make of yourself a mother you've read about in guidebooks:
  a McKinley, a Denali.

But what if the child's too early, if it   might die—

how could she not withdraw herself again

and wait for you to be a harbinger of yourself,
hold you only when it was clear you'd stay?

Spring, sprung. Your thoughts drift today from penance

to the barbecue and back again.
When the rain hits the Weber kettle,
it tolls.

Despite a freezer full of wild salmon,
sometimes for her you'll fast and watch yourself not eat.

You watch yourself walk until you stumble under the weight of
watching

and hear her words when her last voice went out
and came to rest on a fine filament called tape:

OK. Turn that off.

Filmy lis moth

(Stephon Marbury)

Ideal: to drive the lane and look for dishes,
to see the open man, give him his bucket.

The one-on-one for which we are now counseled
blueprints a perfect symmetry that's hard to hold.

Like my friend who dreams of his ex
and wakes to find a moonlit lawn of deer.

In our nightly houses
the dolls insist that we are faithful to ourselves.

When I wake up in a bad mood,
I wonder why my point ignores my shooting guard.

This realm of giving, this realm of reciprocity:
I need a Mr. Make-It-Happen,

a deus ex machina, an all-star
down among us who deigns to fix our gears.

Until then, these reuptake inhibitors are splendid,
as when I find myself a deer on some strange lawn,

my garden-party head a promiscuity of maps
with toll-free grassy lanes and cul-de-sacs.

(The Outskirts of Agnes)

That we sag with many weights
and buoy ourselves with the word—
although the word fails its captain

many a time and to/for no avail—
we of the lesser rank do toil:
take a town like Agnes

with its fine people and subpar soil,
its metal gate and burnt red brick
with a clutch of blue-gray lichen spin.

All night a mayor's words echoed in my head
and wanting this language myself
and others much like me

found the outskirts of Agnes
and I swear our clapping came like rain.
There were stairs past heavy doors

on shrill hinges and finally a window
looking out over a town,
still Agnes, perhaps, all but lights

now and our eyes tracking out to lights' end
where water lays a black tarp—
where captains look east and want,

out of the blue, their little red-red.

(Upanishads)

I trust initial states, my mental Delaware:
as parting snows will downy up the dirt beds,
impatient daffodils debut their taxi silks.
One imagines a garden of dormant lilacs,
dried rattle bags of Columbine, spring ready.

All this among the winter head games—
an old man in his Pisan compound, worse,
in his own head—a diplomatic endgame,
Muoio perché non posso morire.

I put the book down and think of blooming,
move my city of nine gates much closer to the window—
the god cannot burn straw before the godhead,
nor can it blow away the selfsame hay—
I think of prayer as a winterspring caesura
and faithfully make hymns for flowerheads
apocryphal beneath the fallen snow.

(My Persephone)

This year the leaves come hard and fast,
Persephone on her way downtown
with her little burlap bag of notes.

In a hinterland's clue-laden season,
each day's a calling card from the great beyond:
let me call this cold, crisp rain your voice,

what makes a go of red and gold
and frosts what once was veined and juiced, good greens.
I feel that voice and remember your hair—

Brilliance. Dizziness. *Sturm und Drang.*
You left and changed the rules by leaving.

Your seizures used to wrap you up in sleep,
and I would keep you company, dumbstruck.
I was a glass of juice, a damp cloth for your head.

Sleep, undirected, was language incontinent,
vowels of delirium gone consonant
in babble like leaves blown from trees.

How to rake and reconfigure what fast
falls down around me yet again?

I was feeling *August* last night, love—
not *regal* or *emperoresque*, just *hazy*
like weather suspended out over the harbor.

13

It was only August in my head;
walking out into your winter wake
I was beside myself when you or one

just like you (Demeter, lamp lit?)
with the warmest hair went by, and for a moment
what I had was a word, a fine word—

the word was *pretty*; it sat on the tongue
for a while, was pleasant, and was gone.

(First Bird without Her)

Kingfisher, one-timer, come-backer, a player:
even as you ready for your own leaving
you toy with your hiatus in our rusty leaves.
Here come your shorter days and the long trip.

What's it like when you hit that water and
your down is a dam between two currents,
one verbing bloom, one nounish blossom,
one heartfelt and the other encroaching
even if of sustenance it makes a loan?

And I feel for the waters, little tourist,
the realm you cover quick as a fresco,
pinpoints multiplied, Sebastian for arrows
when fish by fish you dive and take your fill.

Like all good sufferers, water underwrites
itself, entry points as brief stigmata,
hardy and forgetful, quick, sharp, and felt,
each instance just as gone as the last.

(Equinox)

I am not pleased with black and white
thinking—obtuse neighbors, the swollen
snowy bowl of the hourglass and brother
black coat on a peg in the dark—yet it governs me.

Allow me my gray matter, my hallways
and stairwells of creaky-speak under night lights
and a voice that might resurrect yet calm
my scared child's freefall of pressing questions.

Was it yesterday or weeks ago when a rain
came so hard and so slant that I nearly wept
while peering through sheets of glass
to the glacial light of an indoor pool
so otherworldly and at pure remove
that I stood outside looking in at the blue?

The romantic wants flowerink and broad daylight,
but June's a dream that speaks when not spoken to,
not a scrapbook ready-made and wish-fulfilled.

I want some clearing or at least an ersatz sun.
My lakeside nephews and nieces: models.
Little balsawood ships of the time being.

(Sweet William)

This evening, you take time and listen to your father's words.
Repeating them or resuming the rounds he made of hallways
cannot tether his younger voice outside your bedroom,
but you can hear familiar hinges from the screen door
and ready for his taillights glowing in your window.

You mistook his silence for sophisticated schemes
of flora that were stained by small blessings
of late afternoon light before evening imperatives
and the moody roost of starlings having settled
once they colored the sky in which they flew.

He made of love few words and slight extensions
not unlike the courtesans who close down dawn,
a restlessness like the roses he bred
to bloom into winter and snow's unsettlement.
Someday your father might be mistaken for flowers

even if there's no immediate need for restoration
or nostalgia's wistful trio of half measures.
Would he have said that you should sing out loud
and find a warbler for yourself, a worthy exception
to emulate that might outshine his lesser traits?

Or do you still make up the words he doesn't say?
Do you pour a glass of easier love to drink,
potential as light that sieves from high trees
and meets the deadlines of your memory
less fractious and lullaby affirming?

Didn't you once pray away all medicine
and lie terribly awake in your child bed
dreading when life would have you no longer?
In between daily rotations and emergencies
flaring like small revolutions from his pager,

wasn't his arrival an occasional harvest
that affirmed you as once-removed from each other?
Sons define themselves away from fathers, but never fully.
Both of you love elsewhere as it burns the here-and-now.
Your father left but never loved his absence; you learned it. ⚡

VOID AND COMPENSATION (2)

(What the Admiral Saw from the Air)

Suppose you're just a little north of the question.
A few degrees east of circumstance.
Miles west of the latke breakfast.

What if the southerlies deflect the river project
and a nor'easter toys with your scavenger hunt?

Do you make a game out of longitude?
Do you sing a little song of latitude,
make up a mantra called locale
and let it resonate out loud and in the head?

Here's what Byrd does:
he keeps his admiral stars in a little box
lined with blue velvet, imitation velvet,
a little northeast of the real deal,
a little west of the real McCoy.

He takes them out from time to time,
lifts up the lid and reacquaints himself with pewter.

And he'll talk to Peary out loud:

You walked where I merely flew.
Your best friend is a dog named Perimeter.

He dreams of Peary on his sled of spent dogs
wrapped in a pair of pure grays, cloak and sky,
sees him stop and skyward raise his hands.

Byrd sits with his boxed stars
and welcomes the white coats of ceremony,
the sharp lapels and the smell of starch,
the pants that have a crease he calls *true north*,
but when he puts his hand upon his chest
his charts are all for naught: the day, *haywire*,
his heart a compass needle gone berserk.

Some stars are given out as praise, others, restitution:
a little north of happenstance, just east of where we'd like to be,
a little west of what's in store and south of expectation.

What does Byrd think when he sees
the real thing, the stars up above,
that burning far away but bright enough to see?

(Meredith Come Back as a Thrush)

Call the clouds *Midwest* or *Magritte*,
they slide in on the last light and soften
the day's harsh bleach into evensong's dusk.
Solstice. Now the days are getting shorter.

So when I see a thrush in the beech out back,
I think *Nightingale*, think *Bright Star* and all that—
but I can't reconcile both truth and beauty.
The prettiest flute from the deep woods
here, playing hooky in the Brooklyn trees?

Memory sings her *now you hear me, now you don't.*
I think of Meredith, who taught me a few things:
Make a weather, make a dust (pestle).
Make a season, make a voice (epistle).
Make of your mouth an embouchure to kiss.

Meredith: welcome back from Los Angeles,
where few walk and buildings can heavy shake.
We used to look each other in the eye and think
(a kind of hear-and-now like Keats' bird),
your singing is bigger than the both of us.

In the last light you're quiet yet still playing
under the should-be stars and their pinprick stops.
You might have wings or a thread around your foot,
can flee or stay branched and teetering in the mind:

that hunch we had about something greater—
it's not the song, nor surety's *just after*,
nor the night trees' slight, dark rustle from the roost—
maybe our larger music is listening.

(Beautiful View)

This here is a town of widows who remain
for some sort of minimal husbandry—
alone, they find themselves again, right here
in the places that their children have left,
riding the warm words of their ministers
like bakery air right out of the clerestory.
They love the recycling truck, its hi-hat vent
making of exhaust more rhythm than blues,
its bones of glass and orphan lids that sing
consumptive songs at every turn and stop.
The industry that they thought broken down
earns fresh red coats of paint and landmark status.
From glass belvederes atop their second houses
they watch the game of nine-lives on the village green
between tourists and locals with sticks and nets.
The attackmen attack. The defenders defend.
Midfielders mediate. It's all so simple in theory.

(Second in Command)

Consider the plight of subordinates, say, Reno,
which drags a bit behind Vegas, or Custer's Rosebud-
crossing Reno, Lakota whipped and glory broke, a xeno-
phobe whose kingdom come was Sioux and Cheyenne flood.

He's called a Queeg for having headed south
and leaving his General with troubles that converge
when reckless captains overcalculate their worth.
They'd rather have lamenting tabloids sing a dirge

on their behalf, so here's a little snack for you, scout:
don't let arrogance drive you up on bridge or bluff;
take a little time to sum up and make out
which routes pass for fortitude and those too tough

given the geometries we plot from positions
on high—fame's runners-up sometimes are sages
provided they meet what they've met with contrition,
if only to cut and cash the future's forgetful wages.

(Sir Parricide)

There is the act, and there is the actor,
Sir Parricide: are you not keenly aware
of your actions, how your first infidelity
was against those who carried you here
in the first place? They were your first place,
and you have butchered them, clear-cut that tract.

If a king is capable of moving backwards,
tomorrow lets you claim what you won't stake today.
One-touch, your thermostat is irrefutable:
set the weather at home as you like it.
Have the heat vents wheeze their intonations
that turn invitation, turn sleep, turn dream.

But wait, your highness, first, a nightcap.
Sir, lager is regal, as are you, your bladder full
so that it might echo your mind, self-served,
so fraught with murky thinking and sharp axes
that you'd piss away a forest into fairway.
See the green? Hear that lone tree, the wind-toy?
Now there's a lark. It's calling. It's your song.

(The Little Flower I Call Kurtz)

So you're related to the iris, in and of its family
that responds to light and gives us, fuzzed and drunk,

an outline, a little tease of what's to come
before the brain, perhaps fuzzed, drunk, sad, ecstatic,

or even undecided and directionless
chances to address whatever shapes appear.

The head welcomes the world and sends ideas to the eye,
which keeps talking. It's open and shut until someone says

Bed, which means it's time for sleep or a season
where I make a case for second and third persons.

I was thinking spring when the nor'easter rolled in
and grated snow down on your optimistic sprigs,

any and all rogue blues that rose before the freeze
now lobby-bound and waiting for their higher power.

The sun can't think yet reasons us perennial—
gives us shorter, colder days, and gradually

grants us more light, a subjunctive spring
until remembering *what ifs* the flowers—

Canary. Reddish purple. The way I remember saffron
or my heart when I cartoon it in my head.

Hard job, small bulb, illuminating up and out of dirt,
pointless, ill-paid, and necessary.

Crocus, the little flower I call Kurtz,
of petals it's none-too-soon to snow in your past tense.

It may be said of pioneers that they have seen
the colors of this world yet call it colorless,

as dirt waiting for us and to happen.

(Annulment with Rhododendrons)

I tried my hardest not to trespass—

went out and learned the garden names by heart
and hushed myself in the presence of spring.

I led wayward bees to open windows,
sent venoms elsewhere for something honeyed.

If friends were down, their troubles were company
on my quarrel walks under sun and moon.

Even my ghosts and I were affectionate.

So when I heard my beloved's voice raised in malice
and saw in either eye a blame or hurt uncauterized,

I felt that moment's measure in my hesitation,
a cold and quiet horse now scaring in its stall . . . .

There never was a bareback virtue
waiting to be broken, was there,

only bread and then my beloved?

We draft from settle down to settlement
as we can't cultivate safekeeping

in either blossoms or the warping
winter cold that furls these finger leaves.

What was our spade and shrub commitment
to the larger goal of greener landscape

fostered intentions so rain-saturated

that we can't take cover; we yield instead
and call this coming down a clearing.

(Lear)

At night I like to leave on all our lamps—
they are investments that prolong the day.
They are expensive. Of sacrifices made
to make this purchase, she says I am not
present, have lost a step. Well, the heart has
in its liquid head a muscle memory;
when it tries to verbalize its grail
one side will always mock the other.

Which is the justice and which the thief,
the marriage as is or the one we imagine?
One's malt that brewers mar with water;
the other's gold ale all happy in its glass.
Still, the smell of restored prairie suggests
fields tended by real persons—not hospice
care behind the heath and its stagecoaches.
When her king of two minds lifts off into flight,
a choral sadness slips loose from his queen.

Both drift and barter simply with themselves.
Poor king, road weary. Watch him suffer small
yet constellated hopes along night interstates,
food, fuel, and lodging as the very pattern
of all patience, not art yet necessary.
Exits would have you believe in company
but yield only pilot lights in houses
of the pious that line the service road.

(Assisted Living)

More has been said about
how relationships don't work

than about how they do.
How do you do?

I walk with you in my head—
walkway and tow-away dovetail

in your skirts and farther in
my head are neednot feelings.

Afeard of hymn, a faineance,
a cleavage, you are from me

a kind of leachate,
fair market, fair catch, fainéant.

This illusory port of you-and-I
needs an animator's patina,

a seminarian on the prow,
a spiritual coxswain.

Listen to my directorial fervor:
too much Billy Wilder has left me

ill-versed for obstinate prompts,
the way you ignore my birthday,

my reprobate barometer too spoon bait,
mints on the pillow as preemptive gestures.

Fair game, fair isle, fair lady—
you build a fence around yourself

of little links: faith, unfaith.
How full I know not how to gauge.

My effete towelette, my sorghum sweet,
where is that handy rustic almanac

of small yet spartan promulgations?
Homesick, I crave a little face-to-face.

So many stories about a girl who for
her boy had big spaces in her heart

only to reshingle the monologue
when siding was the cheaper option.

If I cannot sing the hymn,
I will make myself a myna with some tympani.

I will emancipate the hearsay,
a private kind of media on their kettledrums.

Mania, sweet mainstay: tout à fait.
Will you envy the calm invoice of prior selves

or will you insist on slowly closing doors
and keeping them shut tight?

A space in my heart, you said,
alchemical convening where we were warm

and bright, where we were present tense.
I rent a little room in Stoke-on-Spent,

your letters to me gray testimony now,
royalists in the solarium who hum of yesteryears.

(New Jim Crow)

Weight him down, O side-stairs, with a freight of legalese
that seals him less in glass and more in storm cloud,
the gray cinders of his thought reflecting and reflected there.

Jailed, he's living all that he has seen and could not see,
what served him parentally as not-knowing
and slow hours forged as glass under an out-there sun.

All weight is a beach that sounds of waves untouchable.
It is static and persistent as a sentence,
a code of some cruel parenting handed down as reprimand.

Man. He's nothing that hasn't been told. And so a story.
It's private and something the state would rather
not deal with and now our greatest agriculture.

What mind, fair one, is not a combine of what's wrought?
Just because he speaks a language doesn't mean he knows it.
And where's the handbook for review and reparation?

What could be darker than these statistics in black ink?
What thick strings? What gutturals out jay-walking
in the air that in the mind turn feathered and blue?

His grief is that of church which should sound otherwise.
The imagination now becomes his mother and speaks of him
in his distant chamber, wicked in a white light.

VOID AND COMPENSATION (3)

(Poem as Aporia between Lighthouses)

Are you lonely there?　　　　　　　*Yes, I want you here.*

*

Welcome, day of hearts on paper, night of
lights that punctuate and propagate the dark.

Honor the boats coming in and going out:

as for reefs and shoals I am as they are, fearful making
and terrifying if all the maps can say is *position doubtful.*

Love's wick floats in a bowl of oil, nightly lit.
Its first light asks one question—*Anyone there?*—

if not of ships or me, then perhaps one another.
One would like to think of oneself as landed gentry,

making in the night air beams as swizzle sticks
that shake and stir the dark drink of evening.

Overhead and overheard: light shot out
loses itself in something greater by the second.

Not quite mid if middling, I'm a distance
between points, half-way undecided by my choices.

Of lookouts, the whaling captains asked their men to sing
out at the tops of their voices—there is music in it:

There she white waters, there she blackskins,
there she breaches, blows, or flukes.

So many trinities where water meets the landed,
crying out to one about an other. Third world.

The lighthouse only suggests an autonomy:
part warning, part bearing, it projects that we need others.

To know where you are in relations.
To know that others are thinking of you, even in the abstract.

It is what children realize their parents have
done for them as long as they can remember.

Boats will come so far, no closer.

*

A mother says to her child, in order to help him
learn to do on his own, *pretend I'm not here.*

She says it when she's tired of answering questions.
She says it so that he might see his independence.

It is a crushing and cursory tutorial.
It is his heart's preparation for memory.

*

I love the lighthouse because it is not human:
it must bear both sides of the relationship.

I don't have to manufacture answers for my beloved,
but I do it in my head all the time. It is a wager, a hedge.

I am trying to open up for what my love says and stands for
when I assume she'll leave me for a younger volunteer.

I have grown up thinking that *knowing* means *trouble*:
if I can stay not knowing, it calls to the competent for help.

Of love I always ask: but will it work—
I speak of the world as if it merely happens to me:)

Weather reflected in windows. Colorless bay waves
that adopt blue light and its orphaned molecules.

What amazes me, god-given or random grant,
are the things of this world that color themselves

with what lies outside of and settles on them.

I love the lighthouse mind: forever colonized by others
and assessments made on behalf of their bearings.

How dear of them to lose all sense of self.
Once manned. Now, no human heart, no human error.

*

A wind-blanched corridor between lights.
A sand bar with its gnarled and stunted trees.

Tonight, I'm here because I need to know myself as not at sea,
more grounded in a light shone out towards others.

I am a little fearful: am I between two houses
or am I one looking at and talking to the other?

Might I lend myself a locomotion they can't have?

It is equally plausible that I must choose one light over another.
It is equally plausible that I am one light and my beloved another.

My indigenous name: Little Wool-over-His-Eyes.
These are choices and I have reservations.

Doubt made Pascal hedge his bets. He bet with his head,
not over it—he made of worry some expressions.

I will begin by admitting that I'm lost.
Which means I've been here before as someone else.

I am not obliged to feign confusion.
It is heartfelt, what wears easily, rubs away at a touch.

Meno asks, *how will you find what remains unknown to you?*
I will ask questions. I will pursue knowing

that the darkness is what we bridge despite ourselves.
It is what we're made for. So to speak. To articulate.

*

Here, beached in the stumbling dusk, are ribs, a wreck,
a heart-cage or hull washed up and bleached clean;

no mariner, foreigner, or Jonah to
be found, rescued, or lost—perhaps I'm him

wrecking myself and my imagined children into being,
a skeletal certainty as driftwood recompense.

In my atrium head I articulate ribs;
I make of them a whaling museum.

Look at how suspended bones above us
kept largesse intact in a fluid home—

how each bone suggests enormity and finite solitude
on which schoolkids might peg their thoughts like coats—

rest them upon the infrastructure of what
was living and writhing, a doppelgänger faith

of kinder execution in its having and being held.
Lost and pure, a saint's articulation of some heaven sent.

This was a mother carrying her calf
that met her maker in the shipping lanes.

The museum of small compensations has possession
of the fetal bones—they will be part of the final display.

The relic bones are out for our betterment, the actual
and what we dream both in and out of it:

the students with their brown bag lunches fawning
skyward underneath the skeletal whales.

Little Pascals, they tuck ecstatic notes
inside their innermost coat pockets.

Or maybe they don't know what to say
or how to articulate what's been put before them.

*

When I was a child I needed someone to teach me how to talk.
There were noises I could not make. I needed help.

I asked for many things, craved allowance,
sought permission in a winter household

but kept turning the word *can* into *tan*,
could only make of want a language of summer.

My articulation still an errancy,
I would like to speak better to others

with fewer omissions and substitutions:

instead of *stick* (as in stay), I get *sick* (as in love).)
With my beloved, *run* comes out as *won*.

And I front—I replace distant consonants
with more palatable, frontal others.

The love I speak is not completely accurate— ⟩ *
sounds from its mouth I'd call distortions

arise in certain words that give me difficulty:
circumstances, separation, providence.

The history of love has a stutter:
b-bucket's got a ho-hole in it.

*

Tonight, between the houses, I've brought a child in my head
not yet articulated: he could be my past or my future

or the child I overheard in the library today,
let's call him Nico (as his mother does),

thrilled and shrill among the prospects
of volumes, all words unspoken and bound,

a beauty impossible to take—and his mom,
articulator, said to him and his noise,

his kicking of blocks in the kids' section
out of their stacks and behind radiators,

We don't do that. You can't, you can't, thank you.
Little Nico, your mother's intentions are best,

meant to make of your strange world a Damascus,
market stalled, that you might navigate on your own.

So when your mother says you should apologize
for kicking blocks in the hall of texts-in-waiting,

where do you find yourself? On the shores of apology
with a stutter, in speech or in thinking, *s-sorry?*

"Nico, you're not listening." *I would like to.*
"You're not cooperating." *I would like to.*

The mother love is unbearable, isn't it, Nico?
You're giving her the Heisman, it's too much

so here's the push-pull that Hoffman says is paint
that makes of love some province-lands better

discovered and let go, a turning off
provided there's a resting place, a child's pose.

A love vindictive when our benefactors
wake us from our selfish ways: if love calls

the I to attention, we turn our cheek
from the beloved, her eyes too much to bear.

It is a distance warranted by knowing
only that they are not fully gone.

*

Nico, ours is a space with privileges
that can and will be taken away from us.

Your sibilant mother wishes to help you figure time.
She talks about how the hands of the clock move.

She will ask, tucking you in later,
about your morning, your afternoon, and your evening.

She's teaching you about sequences:
Do we pay for groceries before we choose them?

Do you put your socks on after your shoes?
Do we read a story after we go to sleep?

It's what these houses do for us, Nico.
They read us nightly even when we're gone.

*

A fourth-order Fresnel lens
manufactured by the brothers Chase:

would Plato call them pessimists or poets,
and would he see the houses as ideal forms?

I love the history of their close attention—
hopes from a promontory born of pessimism

that yields in warning a better than dead-reckoning
sense of where the sea-weary sit, how they might dream

of home and their beds that can rock and lie still,
in motion from the rise and fall of ribs, not waves.

Nico, I'm trying to pretend you're here
so that we might save each other

the way these solitary houses do, distant
but diligent in their need of others.

Shhhhh, said your mother, *people are thinking.*
Their voices are in their heads and behind the covers of books.

Someone had a hammer and a saw. Someone saw through
the forest for the trees and where their absence might lead us.

They built a church and it became a library.
Some foreign mariners called themselves saints

of arrivals and departures, imagined
and articulated both a future grace

that walked quietly behind their will and
a plan to unfold where once was nothing.

We call them parents.

*

For the next few years, Nico, it is your job
to play, to pretend you are not here.

Simone says uproot yourself and
see a landscape as if you are not there.

Soon enough you'll navigate Damascus
and walk its stalls without the bag lunch,

without the field trip, a Tunis,
or perhaps more local, a Providence.

This could be a coast for Aeneas and
his bone-weary men, Mercury a kind

of lighthouse making Carthage open up
its arms for those who'd hurt, who'd love and leave.

It's sad but true that every bridge suggests
its own burning, Nico: we all take leaves.

Kinnell called love *the wages of dying*,
but we invest that feeling, more wager than wages:

I've felt that love and let it go, have
only approached the clerks at the windows

with my program and my penciled hunches.
You'll wager one day, little man,

little prince of the paramutual window,
you'll have your stakes and your downs and your derby.

Think of Pascal. These bets are the notes that sow and sew;
keep them close to your heart in your little pea coat.

✓ ⟮Love is pitch and tar and twine for your boats
⟮of consolation and compensation.

Try not to fill the emptiness in yourself
by creating one in someone else.

Someone foreign. Some beloved.

One day you'll leave, and they'll live in your absence.
In your future present-tense, be a little less gone.

*

These houses barter small talk on floes of big thinking;
it's beautiful in the way that the fallen recognize each other.

My beloved sends me a zebra finch
whose notes compose demand and ransom,

the way a winter cardinal encounters
the cloud-gray scale of a cold front

and cracks it with its *chip*, a stepped-on glass
and blood-red plumage saying mazel-tov and

making of suffering something acknowledged.
Then the front clears. Then we come out of the blue.

If we find ourselves at temple doors, attendance
and speech might make us feel churchlike.

Flightless yet winged.

*

Pretend I'm not here—it sounds terrifying
as words between a parent and child.

Between anyone. It's what we might say
to ourselves for our children imagined into being,

amongst ourselves, no matter how boatless
these seas, no matter how fogged or fucked up.

Half-baked on what's hardly terra firma between houses,
the cedars appear stunted by their preacher winds.

Is it pity or guilt you feel with these trees
and the orchard in your head that sows them?

Call the barrens between houses useless and harmless.
What listens now in unmanned buildings is my godhead—

my loss, my errancy, and my dunes
becoming larger than my knowledge of them.

Pretend I'm not here: easy for the beacons by day
before dusk scares them into necessary speech.

Think of an articulationist teaching
a mute to utter what can be understood,

the dental plaster cast conveying
a desire for more perfect occlusion:

as in, you need to close off and shut down
in order to be understood.

Any gestures into darkness have radical lenses
that fire, fan out, go silent when sun rises

and highlights bones washed up on the beach,
picked clean by gull, decreated by kittiwake.

What of wings articulated to a body, how to teach oneself
and one's child that rot is what happens in a chrysalis?

How can I say that to a beloved who's flown?

Can a couple articulate ribs around themselves,
bang on the bars as wardens, fearful of departures?

Lighthouses, holdovers lovely in your obsolescence,
we use our own stars that we find despite cloud cover:

idols for idolaters, unmanned yet functioning,
your spoken oath our brightest apparition.

*

If the sea could sing itself a Providence,
some citizens unschooled in drifting

would hang onto their cargo of dusk
and look for promissory notes of light.

It is a wishful thinking, how petals
and not seeds might articulate the rootstock.

As for running with hares and hunting with hounds,
are these infidelities acoustic or spoken?

Such is the gap and faith in loss as loam
out of which the wind-ripped trees seem to curl

and whose fingers either rise up in prayer
or aim the blame like plosives through the beachgrass.

We had put our hearts down on paper.

We had a mouthful of tools for occlusion
and stalled fronts to bring rain when speech failed.

It would be great if you could come here, she said.

I didn't.

There are myths and idolatry and not showing up.
Ways of seeing more clearly. Of hurting.

*

If I've only found faith in loss
and measured commitments in distance,

I still have thoughts of reconciliation:
that I might speak as the houses would,

that I might stutter love and make it fluent.

The hope of interiors as seen from a distance.
A memory of beloveds as a Passover,

no longer recollection from far-and-away
but reenactments, cups and plates and rituals.

Here is where these houses faithfully
urge compassion in the face of distance.

They know our tendencies, say, with ants and horses:
we step on the former and bet on the latter.

*

What would I tell an older Nico who wants
to man the houses, a superintendent of lights?

To keep the wicks trimmed, the chandeliers dusted,
the clean glass chimneys fitted free from smoky points?

For fresh air, keep the leeward vents open
and for memory keep a journal of ships passing?

I would tell the younger man that
it's okay to be a little blue.

It means he's filled with scattered light,
what hasn't finished its trip, disperses

or gets lost, perhaps separated from us
down here between these two lighthouses.

Like Patinir's *Saint Jerome*, from a distance
his blues in the very backs of his horizons

and also in his heart, worn on his sleeve,
as if he were draped in his own distance.

Hello, Jerome. Thank you, Nico, but now
I need to say this to myself and my beloved:

I'm sorry that I keep you at bay.

For the monotony of *what if?* beamed out
as a broadside for living. You and me,

even if you and I are impossible,
mere lights that reach out from our anchorage.

I was a child with best intentions standing
between my parents with their separate lamps

and even now I'm not confident whether
I'm for myself or from confusion—

by day a lighthouse part of bigger pictures,
at night online and speaking in threads.

But now I am here. Trying to be here.

*

In the broadcasts from Providence,
the singers are something of an abstraction,

an ideal remote and only imagined near.
No solid objects here refuse to declare themselves,

not brotherly fog horns and their droning moan
nor the eider sisters in their coats of down:

theirs is a will uneasy with absence
like a man who makes himself a boy again

so as to speak gently and contemplate
the darkness between beacons

and what it might be like
to enter the presence of the fixed and lit.

Articulators of bone, occlusions of speech,
while I bear my coats and layers, half deed, half dream,

I'm still here, my feet between these houses.

It must mean that I accept that hallowed ground
might very well rise up and wreck me.

*

Are you lonely there?   *Yes, I want you here.*

VOID AND COMPENSATION (4)

(This Night Different than All Others)

Strange birds, my love and I, such different wings
and you should see the horse we rode in on:

his name is *Avatar*, mindful of jockeys
as he sucks on salt and craves his sugar cubes.

We would like of spring a spring concert,
the oboes firm in the woodwind thickets.

My tulip love once made the larger abstracts handy,
even present—small beds tended and color-fast.

In these few days where we eschew our bread
and wean kids from their mother's milk (pareve)

what's pew and testament turns domestic.
We fill out forms in order to adopt

before the great spirit flies over our house—
the great flyby, the choosing of some chosen.

(Facebook)

My friends who were and aren't dead
are coming back to say hello.

For the most part, they seem successful.
They have children, which I can only imagine.

The hairy kid we called *Aper*, I haven't heard
from him and wonder if in every contact

there are apologies inherent
for feelings hurt and falling out of touch—

I'm sorry in the way that dogs out back
bark at the nothing they're trying to name.

Now and then the missing turn up
and we speak to one another in threads

more kind than faces posted downtown
when tower dust settled and sky went blue again.

When Leo died we couldn't believe he wasn't hiding,
that his laugh would not sound out, announce his return.

What a laugh. Goofy. His. Purely his
and out loud like a dog barking at stars.

Something heavenly. An application
against insults or the immanent unheard.

That was Leo. And he left.
I don't think he meant to go

before he found some beloved and made
someone in and not of his image.

I want to find Leo in the spill;
I want to discover that he's a chemist

and tell him it's like high school all over
with so much living, it was nice, to be done

and to see and hear from you after so long.
You seem great. You look exactly the same.

(Tenochtitlán)

She wanted to know where he was—
how he spent his time, which horses held
up better in the foreign climate.
And did he think of her at all when seeing
fabulous wildflowers or local women.

The breath from his cartographer's assistants
cannot dry the maps as quickly as he'd like.
He'd like to send one home, a keepsake;
he'd like to remember this city to her
before his torch-bearing men tear it down.

If his faith can lay a kingdom to waste,
then he'll need perpetuity forthwith
more than her voice inside his reliquary head.
The question that she's asking is his own:
what will we build on what we have razed?

Of change, maps offer mute testimony;
the maiden and the married names appear
intaglio above the doorbell *Cortés*.
Affirmer of dominions, it hardly rings,
a maquette of corresponding silence.

Cartography can't tell him where he's going,
only what he saw and was, a moment of his knowing.
And since his tense is always changing or has changed
(a reminder, a memory, a casualty of mastery),
a place he's never been will better suit him.

Cartographers, make haste—of present tense
please make for him an archive of his holdings.
Building a city on a former's cooling ashes
requires hindsight that forswears
second-guesses and sweet talk from better halves—
her atlas and not his moral compass.

(Childless)

Overload, this floral mark of May, her post-shower
sky-bound bust-up of dirt beds tended and called out in love.

A joy lot, a dream going deep; June, the fly pattern,
the bee season, a chalk-talk in pollen, the hook and trail;

petal beds abuzz in flux, July-ripe, tensile, and tonic—
the hummingbirds of needle and lobe; lid-flutter and lash-lush—

and August's deep seat, catbird mew and tangled underbrush,
the wayward come-ons, the cicadas dropping hints.

I hear their choral rush of rattle-tales, shed skin and dense sweat,

the laying down and loosing of old selves like trousers,
hip and buck, the mind lily-bent and lamb-eared for real.

Damned by scent I've left half my heart
attached to my prick, my sting—what a stink

I've made of love and leaving—a law followed,
a script shade, fallow, ghost-written, fancy-less:

our hearts, our choices, our chill, our childing,
our elevation out of ranks shortlived.

(On Reading)

for Larry Levis

1.

When I read in bed, the book above me
held high, arm extended, I hold
the top right corner with my left hand
and let the finished pages rest on my wrist—
as if I'm denying the rays of a small sun
or keeping the printed word at bay.
It's Chekhovian, how everything descends,
the protagonists, their stars and their sun.
This morning it's my friend: I haven't learned
to say his name in death since what he left
of his life on paper—tuberculin ink
spit up and out as darker rubies that
his body couldn't keep and went to pages—
stains that snow crystal-by-crystal, persistent
and held above the head and kept at bay.

2.

It's Valentine's Day and I'm reading in bed.
I'm with my lover and we're breaking up
although neither of us knows it yet—
I am reading and she is sleeping.
The book is still above me but I'm gone
(prescience disguised as daydreaming):
I'm at my lover's apartment years later
and I'm holding her baby, not mine and yet
a ruby of my making, my ambivalence.
Love's less and less about someday and more
of a resuscitation of someone—
come, friend or lover and child fast asleep;
come, dawn, all clock-tick and sparrow-chatter
and daylight starch waiting for ink and wanting—
the books are by the bed, and they are dead and ready.

(Bake McBride)

A constitution is a snowy field in a suburban library:
my friend reads poems from his middle age
to a noon audience with white hair, a field in thaw.

Here, a little sprig with snow shifting there
and falling away, words out over a meadow
ready for migratory daydreaming.

The ladies fly miles away from Matthew,
his warm notes that resonate and spring
from his mouth and further thaw the snowy field,

his voice offering *Barcelona, Oolong,*
armistice, Positano, a young bride
making apple crisp on her wedding day.

Maybe one listener dreams herself in Spain
or fancies a scone, one thinks of Pershing,
one is Ariel over the Amalfi coast,

and the old lady in me turns major league,
remembers Bake McBride, who, wicked fast,
ran down line-drives, drew walks, and stole bases.

Later, outside the library from my car,
I watch a man in a yellow vest direct traffic
and a yellow bus take someone else's kids home.

And in the mirror I see silver, first visible
in chin stubble, has migrated to my temples.
It means in my mythology that I should hear

gravel under my wheels at night, a housewarming;
find morning frost on my windshield and rid
gray rime from my sight; wave to the window-child

waving back; and feel her mind not moving
from that porthole starboard to the street,
until evening comes and fathers walk through doors.

But it's afternoon here, with trees like traffic lights
having left from green and summer's go
to autumn's orange and arresting reds, caution

signs to see the world before it runs: Bake's on first,
checking out the finger-and-limb semaphore at third
from a coach going gray who once ran without stopping.

(Prosopopeia)

First was nothingness and then its music,
your voice a Texas having formed itself
inside a house surrounded by dark trees,
a room entirely vulnerable at night.

External stairs led right to your balcony:
would that they felt more like opportunities
to break curfew and leave the sullen household
instead of steps of predatory thinking.

Out of that wood I did not know I'd come
to labor through the rhododendrons
so late in life and find you there, a love
whom I would fly to and yet threaten.

Love, you need to know I felt those fears
and blew them off as signs of bad intent.
The false eyes on my paper wings were
meant to ward the others off, not you:

I did not falter at the pool nor fall
for any light that spoke as if it knew
my name, yet some thorn caught my sleeves, brought on
a downright wicked helicoptering.

From the darker yard I see another light,
neon thin, blue vertical in its small cage.
Its crackling repartee is killer, a laugh
track of staccato bursts and briefer stops.

It is not singing yet suggests your voice,
rehab and all its slang imperatives.
If I get over my grounding, I'll get there.
I'll find my way in and burn what I've been.

(Pug-Nosed Dream)

If most things speak for themselves, can't it be said
that really you're doing the thinking for them?

Consider our obsession with exclusion:
a cold front comes in and forces you to hunker down
as other migrants wing their way to some gold coast
with enough fat in their chests to burn down a barn.

Isn't your own heart that way from what or whom you can't have?
Wasn't Sarah Vaughn singing this all along?
Polka dots and moonbeams, for sure, and that dress
that loves your body put aside, and that touch,

oh brick wall, oh tin car, oh small space
inside the crumple zone of either/or.

(Drone)

Majesty, when you start lobbing statistics,
I feel a little like an understudy.

Granted, the water is what we thirst for.
Granted, the rain has been limited.

But your calculations, who are they?
Manipulated figures, subjects chosen,

ordinals merely mown like a lawn
whose clippings won't fly far from the blade?

I know the hive's incendiary dances.
I can't get sent home; I am home.

We men are minor subsidies, buy-backs.
My company—practically banished—of little

labor hums an idle music, *Adagio*,
dazed and taking in warm sun like junk.

I miss my mother's thermos full of meaning:
its coming back meant I was cared for.

I thought enough lint from capital's loom
might yield some robes to make a man,

but for flowing, only the sun remains
insistent, affluent, and even-keeled.

About flowers, your women won't stop talking
in that elfin compass thrum of wild potential.

I hear the meadows are a riot—
Allegro, white noise from a freeway hewn.

(Prima Facie)

Little sugar maple, you've lost your head
from the top down, most of your rustle intact
yet fated—the autumn winds are moving.

Who can blame you? We're all manufactured
in facilities that process lunacy—
you're not the first poet to lose a grip.

Even the willows get iced by chill's slander:
Old Jack's a delegate of loneliness
who relegates all bonds a May away.

September, October, and November
hand down writ summonses to chlorophyll
as augured by the waxwing's reminders:

Remainder, let winter call and confirm
the stone's throw from your summer rental.
Faith, little tree. Trust your science pedigree.

Solve the stormy aftermath: umbrella sums
of broken stems, twisted ribs, and canopies
shorn from their sheltered intentions. Then sun.

(When She Doesn't Talk to Me)

I'm ten again and can't bear love's word-
less quiet, bigger-than-I'll-ever-be

quiet, my gut feelings a panic
of sincerely calculated error.

How ought one scramble up that tricky scree?
A bushel and a peck and a hug around the neck?

Hurt, the lovely albatross, belongs
on a wind rarely landed, but who

won't get winded on such thermals and fall
right out of flight, right out of that madness?

My longing throws a little search party
whose playlist is a choral rondeau

of Fortunately / Unfortunately—
such strophes are taken for granted

but really I'm making them, like my dreams.
What I have makes way for what I'm wishing.

As with childhood toys,
objects and affections towards longing.

As when I'm ten and can't bear
what's underneath not talking.

I can't name it. As in, *it's raining*.
Actor and action—who or what

verb, because the state of being
is jealous and wants its complement.

I like the linking verb, the way
it suggests an otherwise,

a child in a rumble seat
wishing his kin were more kind.

When my mother died, I received a letter
I'd written to her; she saved it, and now

from time to time I'll take it out
and read the archaeology

of wandering cathedrals
and meals taken and clouds moving

across a landscape that we shared.

A thin blue airmail letter
and no more talking, unkind providence.

VOID AND COMPENSATION (5)

(Waxwing Icarus)

I trust the waxwing—its liberty
will come with its corruption.
A keeper of coffee-colored feathers,
I have my father's funds in a swale beyond
the nesting trees and phone wires sans dialogue
that no longer thrum my small, clawed feet.
Think about a folded wing for long enough
and soon a host of motivations will unfurl:
primaries, secondaries, then flight that renders
you wireless towards a nest of your own.
Stop seeing your reflection as a rival.
He's not so august, and neither are you.
Family and migration are two-way streets:
one day is chilly and the next gives you thermals.
I, too, once had a father by my side—
he's gone because I left him.

(Migraine)

for Allen Grossman

Here's a side effect that's very front and center:
I am forgetting the words for things. It's not a matter

of mistaking the Ash for the Linden, of conjuring
the chickadees to my hand from the Arrowwood.

They are a certain kind of medicine like the image
of the beech leaves moving in a wind I cannot hear.

My head-hurt, that crush of pebbles in a tin pan,
it's still for the moment—but not my forgetting.

That's closer to home—opaque and gauzy-drunk.
There is a bowl in the dish drain; it has holes in it.

I use it to wash the greens that come out of the ground.
I use it to let water run away.

What do you call that drain inside the other drain?
Words arrive like spores from other worlds tried on and out.

And although I talk to myself like snow
in evergreens or blackbirds on wires

I know not what I'm looking through to see—
this help I need, in deed, in trust—what is it called?

I'm reading a poet who is building a boat for his death—
in love with his fading mind and what he has left of it.

It is inside his head and looks out at stones
on a beach and remembers his mother, ideas

like a chest and some ribs and something
plush and heaving in that space, ideas

like God and the winds of heaven that come here
to move the birch and beech leaves, then remove them.

(Reading Beckett in Saratoga)

Do you look beyond your choices at their worst,
        née urged-up, née caught-on-rail, née weakened,

and hope they'll match their pedigree, or worse,
        bet by name or the petal-pretty jockey silks?

Beyond the grandstand crammed with hoi polloi,
        handicappers beautiful in either

our bravura or our mental polio,
        lie groves and fake lakes as in-kind consolations.

Feeling game and fading late, a nice life
        outside the grounds, doesn't work for thoroughbreds

whose trinity—win, place, or show—unnerves.
        Either you love or you don't, he writes.

Poor footing compels more studying between
        the bugled interventions of post times.

I tend to hedge. I box the exactas.
        As if I were the profit, not the risk.

Such a human world, wearying yet craved,
        these half-hearted choices writ in pencil

with spent tickets down like leaf-litter
        shuffled and kicked-through on the clubhouse floor.

Last race, a wise guy drops back yet rallies
        past the chalk and the tired full field—

the lines murmur and tempers dislocate
        over gut feelings and past performances.

If I have broken awkwardly, swung wide,
        claimed *I could have done with other loves, perhaps*,

and can vaguely remember a great match
        (a ruffian, a foolish pleasure),

it would be nice to break inside, hold sway;
        show tactical speed, save ground, and draw clear.

But what I wish for as they load the gate
        and wait to start merely sets the odds.

And they're off.

(Field Guide)

Page one's a white space for thinking

even here among the evergreens
beyond the living room and the white noise.

The guide held firmly in the hand means to see—

through mist and wind made visible by branches,
do you name a thing and lose other options, counterlives?

Are you in turn a season named and filled with music?
Say then the weather changes and takes the singing elsewhere?

Of fidelity and proximity, the latter is a watchword.

A window. A looking out through lenses
that magnify and conjure up an other
in your place or by your side. Two forms. Two matters.

From expectations of pure pop in flowering trees
down to knee-high scrub, with hope and faith
I tried to come to terms with what was common.

I heard and sang back a little brown bird:
Wish-wish, my little clay-color, coo.

I tried to name what I saw and how I felt
and map a purple hurt as presence through winter.

And then that bird was gone. Or the song,
or the singing, and what's left

is a field where birds might happen:
a mind between living room and evergreens,

a blind so we first see without being seen—
not mentioned in books, found only in looking.

(Good Friday)

Here come the cherubs with their watering cans,
this after a very modest amount of beer
and still there's dirt beneath my nails.
The cuticle moon and her hangnail light
can barely brush my planted asters,
little purple dividends all Byzantine
up against a plain of pale wainscoting.
What if you lived in a dark bed
just outside a sacred house: what would you
do for some caretaking, a bit of tending?
Would you and your petals wait for rain,
or would you simply wither yourself down,
break yourself up until you were almost a shade
and so desirous of resurrection you'd cry out
for your winter bed of dead and dying leaves?
Would you think of the nymph Saturday
on the outskirts of reverence, beloved Sunday?

(Rand McNally)

On the road of oleanders turning to men I remained sad
for I knew my solitude would sabotage Mom's carpool.

On the road of bougainvillea getting manly I was still green,
and so I walked while others rushed ahead.

What could I do with my visibility limited,
my time, of the essence? Here's an essence for you—

adolescence. Just a bunch of amped-up boys
with laminated menus floral-wide and chock-full.

I revised quietly. I was lay-low, no butterfly:
would that grace and fear made Churchills of us all.

And on the road of gardenias now men, I sustain
a daylight savings and wait for headlights

to jewel the road signs, the gem words
telling me what and where and how far.

(Realtor)

If we take stock of plain truths, my presence
here and yours there, and consider what kind
of gravel we might use to pave a path

and join the twain; if the measure of our power
to abstract ourselves becomes a kind of labor day
where we morph yet table talk of changes,

then what might we make of our love?
An imagined vireo once known
as *Solitary*, professorial and flown?

In the rented yard I hear a cavalry
of half notes, wagons circled, a House Wren
singing the green home we might have built.

Back-bush prophet, little trash-talker
who scolds and composes us as rainclouds,
he monologues for leafing and blooming.

Above the grounded and their boundary fences
come intentions and territories wingéd—
I hear songs all morning worth following:

tourist notes necessarily tethered
to an august apparatus, they rise
above property and make of the air

a most excellent canopy of rights.

(Cardinalized)

Up in the morning and the scenery all Dutch
with wind, gray cloud, a scrim of kept pigeons flying
their kite language in tight cursive on invisible lines.
Everything else—the boats, the harbor whitecaps,
the sky out east where sun fights through—is *what not*.
Feeling half-empty, I want my looking
to either worry or reel the birds back in.

I can flood any landscape with anxiety
about choosing a future with somebody:
every crush feels sky-blue before clouds appear
and give the company I keep the sound of wings,
the pulleys and levers and strings of flight.
I'd rather not wake up feeling Dutch all over and say
You don't close the barn door after the horse is gone.

I try a pomegranate on my plate.
The red-on-black speaks cardinal
because history is winged and has a fast heart,
just like the bird in my throat wrapped in silk,
a voice so full of longing it could hush a church.
I want that kept cardinal out—give *what not*
flight and hear it turn *what if*, sung loud.

Imagine an entire college of cardinals
deliberating the next papacy,
how in their choosing they signal in black smoke
that theirs is a mind gone chimney making
robes for the air to defrock and unthread.

That windowless chapel full of cardinals
that ponder their way towards white smoke:

What if they could hear their flock of namesakes?
What if the men in robes could see themselves
in flight for a moment and like how it feels?
What if they heard that? What if they went there?

(Two Narratives of Longing)

1.

There's a freight train in my fridge—
for real, I'm not talking about malt liquor
or brand names and the vistas they unfurl.
Sure there's a Longtrail or six, hops and malt,
plus a few Blue Moons and an Ocean Spray
that's never met a shore where it could settle
and Tabasco waiting on the lucite
above the crisper where peppers go soft.
But when the motor kicks in for cooling
it sounds like a locomotive up to speed
and halfway through its plains and darker woods.
I can't go near the door when it's running:
if I light that landscape's gas lamps, I'd die
if an open door revealed only juice or jam
where tracks and travel and curling smoke
might be heading off to greener pastures.
And if I phone you across town right now
maybe I'll hear it pass by your window
and wonder what kind cargo it might carry:
my heart packed in salt, my cauliflower mind
non-stop stoked to hop a freight and backtrack
from its purchase to its ideal first field.

2.

There's a schooner in the middle of the library—
I'm serious. It's been christened and raced
(see the faded photos on the back stairwell),
a grand banks schooner named Rose (your middle name)
that can smell the salt from where she's interred
in the main hall of an old church half-filled with books
that a kid might love if only his parents kept reading.
You were always more reader than sailor
even in your leaving, a film brief and grainy
the way my winter mind imagines summer.
All that half-scale longing in a library—
the schooner a stone's throw from water
it won't navigate and all those words in waiting
truer than a compass in a call-girl's chest.
Mary says more people come for the boat
than the books, even as I check out twelve.
I don't wince when tourists use their flashes
but I wonder about all words under cover
and whether they long for the light of day,
to flock out from their spines all eager for
an iris and pupil that can carry them away.

(Éminence Grise)

Wind, what will you wield this given day—
each wave and grain that calls you lord?

What influence exerted miles from here
will turn dunes and send longspurs into flight,

let February's gray ministers roll in, each
considerably less known than his nation?

Confident or confidant, the sun in her habit of clouds
is a small red ball, a conspiracy of sun.

I think of her and sit in her studio,
a shelter, a harbor where longing

navigates, either tethered or tillered,
the figuring of three dimensions into two.

I'm one agent who's been cast underneath
what's overcast—we're in a game of jacks.

Small sun socked in a gray pocket, come out;
then set yourself as you wish and bring night down.

Lay out what needs to be said, silver and stainless,
then gather us like stars in time with your ascent.

Let's make the studio sought after, where you and I
under a honeycomb quilt might linger and lie down.

To lie down with the painter, she-lion and she-lamb,
to touch the hands that lay down beds of jacks,

stars for gathering, is to hazard and pledge
we have the means to clear the sky of clouds.

(Just as They Come)

Call the figure in the trees jay or Jew,
I'm him. I have a house that smells of lemons;
when the going gets tough the air turns citrus.

The sun-kissed, she's a friend of mine, and I,
dutiful bird, do follow her from limb to limb—
I take whatever air my meager lungs can hold.

I cough, I think of Kiev. My elders
make a garden of old country, but I dream
of torches, horsemen, and rage bearing down on me.

Do they murmur *talis qualis* even in their sleep?
The winds of change play part and parcel with my days,
my tallith feather-light, my hinges cerulean blue.

When I was a fledgling I grew fond of pears,
would stake out promiscuous trees, the orchard
where petals above thick-grown grass were jazz.

That was a music I fell down in front of, spent,
and you want a set of wings like mine, cheap?
I say to you, take care twice with what you crave—

a bird that's flown might covet your body
to ground itself on two strong feet and sing
hosannas to dirt and salt in the new world.

Watch this jay hop down from branch to branch,
his plumage is a fire called blue and I am he:
I'm ink for Ezekiel, my cry a *get-ready*:

I'm here to trade my wings for a solid set of ribs,
look up at my steeple trees, know where I've been,
walk the walk, and grant the birdless their wings.

Notes

"(My Ear, My Alabama, My Monk)" — I once heard Cornelius Eady talk about Monk's playing as "elbows and knees" — thanks to him for that idea.

"(Tsimtsum)" — The concept of Tsimtsum comes from Jewish mysticism and considers how God, who is everywhere, needed to withdraw in order to make the space in which the world could then be made.

"(Stephon Marbury)" — Stephon Marbury was the point guard of the New York Knicks from 2004-2009.

"(Upanishads)" — *Muoio perché non posso morire*: I die because I cannot die.

"(What the Admiral Saw from the Air)" — 1909, Robert E. Peary claimed that he was the first to reach the North Pole. Richard Byrd claimed to have been the first to fly over the North Pole in 1926.

"(Second in Command)" — Marcus Reno was a major in the Seventh Cavalry under the command of George Armstrong Custer at the Battle of the Little Bighorn in 1876. Reno's unit survived the battle, but he got heavy flak for failing to come to Custer's aid.

"(New Jim Crow)" — The poem plays off "Madame la Fleurie" by Wallace Stevens and was inspired by Michelle Alexander's *The New Jim Crow*.

"(Poem as Aporia between Lighthouses)" — Wood End and Long Point Lighthouses, Provincetown, MA. Other locales include the New Bedford Whaling museum in New Bedford, MA, and the Provincetown Public Library, located in what was once the Center

Methodist Episcopalian church and which houses a 66-foot half-scale model of the fishing schooner *Rose Dorothea*. Thanks to Carlo Ginzburg and Rebecca Solnit for inspiration.

"(Facebook)" – This poem is for Leo Schaeg Millar, class of 1988, Oberlin College.

"(Bake McBride)" – Arnold Ray "Bake" McBride was Major League Baseball's National League Rookie of the Year in 1974.

"(Prosopopeia)" is for Kim France.

"(Prima Facie)" – Prima Facie translates to "at first sight" or "at first look"; it refers to a lawsuit or criminal prosecution in which the evidence before trial is sufficient to prove the cause unless there is substantial contradictory evidence presented at trail.

"(When She Doesn't Talk to Me)" – Thanks to Mark Svenvold for the *it* in "it's raining."

"(Reading Beckett in Saratoga)" is for Matt Rasmussen and for Maggie Estep.

"(Éminence Grise)" is for Leslie Murray. The title translates as "gray eminence" (originally Père Joseph, Cardinal Richelieu's confidential agent/monk, for the gray habit he wore in contrast to the Cardinal's red habit.)

"(Realtor)" is for Gabriela Salazar.

"(Cardinalized)" is for Matthew Lippman.

Acknowledgments

This book is for my brothers, Stephen, Christopher, and Matthew; and for my parents, Carol and William. Without you, nothing.

Thanks to the editors of the following publications in which many of these poems, some in slightly different versions, were published: *A Public Space*, *Agni*, *The American Poetry Review*, *Bomb*, *The Canary*, *Colorado Review*, *From the Fishouse*, *The Hat*, *The Iowa Review*, *jubilat*, *The Literary Review*, *The Lumberyard*, *Ploughshares*, *Seneca Review*, *Shankpainter*, *Sixth Finch*, *Spinning Jenny*, *The Texas Observer*, *Tin House*, and *The Best American Poetry, 2012*.

Love and thanks: Kirsten Andersen, Kathleen Bacon-Greenberg, Catherine Barnett, Christian Barter, Deborah Bernhardt, Suzanne Bottelli, Kim Burwick, Tina Cane, Cort Day, Erica Ehrenberg, Kim France, Stuart Friebert, Jim Galvin, Forrest Gander, Regan Good, Joanna Goodman, Jorie Graham, Beth Harrison, Edward Hirsch, Brigid Hughes, Henry Israeli, Ted Jones, Sara Eliza Johnson, Larry Levis, Rebecca Lindenberg, Amy Margolis, Diane Mehta, Heather McHugh, Leslie Murray, Sarah Rose Nordgren, Peter Petas, Minna Proctor, Margaret Reges, Sam Reed, Don Revell, Gabriela Salazar, Anne Sanow, Marisa Schwartz, Heidi Jon Schmidt, Salvatore Scibona, Roger Skillings, John Skoyles, Tom Sleigh, Bruce Smith, René Steinke, Gerald Stern, Mark Svenvold, Melissa Tuckey, Diane Vreuls, David Wojahn, Lawrence White. And Betty.

My grateful appreciation for support, time, and space go to the Fine Arts Work Center in Provincetown, The MacDowell Colony, the Corporation of Yaddo, I-Park, Art OMI/Ledig House, Willard R. Espy Literary Foundation, UCross Foundation, Millay Colony, and Vermont Studio Center. Thanks to the Ethical Culture Fieldston School for leave time and for the lively hearts and minds of my students and colleagues. Thanks also to Nick, Robyn, Josh, and Lynn for making this book happen.

Michael Morse lives in Brooklyn, New York. He teaches English at the Ethical Culture Fieldston School.